W9-AVW-803

Caribou

And Reindeer, Too

by Joyce Markovics

Consultant: Dr. Anne Gunn
Caribou Biologist

BEARPORT
PUBLISHING

New York, New York

Credits

Cover and Title Page, © Donald M. Jones/Minden Pictures/Getty Images; TOC, © Robert Harding Picture Library/SuperStock; 4, © John E. Marriott,wildernessprints.com; 4-5, © John E. Marriott,wildernessprints.com; 6, © Daniel J. Cox/Natural Exposures; 7, © Alaska Stock/NGS Images; 9, © Fritz Mueller Photography; 10, © Dennis Fast/VWPics/SuperStock; 11T, © Richard H. Smith/Photo Researchers, Inc.; 11B, Courtesy Leanne Allison and Karsten Heuer/necessaryjourneys.ca; 12T, © age fotostock/SuperStock; 12B, © Glenn Oliver/Visuals Unlimited, Inc.; 13, © Accent Alaska/Alamy; 14, © Nigel Bean/Nature Picture Library; 15L, © Gary Schultz/AlaskaStock; 15R, © Ron Sanford/Photo Researchers, Inc.; 16, © Heather Meader-McCausland/hmmphotography.com; 17, © Fritz Mueller Photography; 18L, © Patrick J. Endres/AlaskaPhotoGraphics.com; 18R, © S. Michael Bisceglie/Animals Animals Enterprises; 19, © Matthias Breiter/Minden Pictures/NGS Images; 20, © Steven Kazlowski/AlaskaStock; 21T, © Michio Hoshino/Minden Pictures/NGS Images; 21B, © Michio Hoshino/Minden Pictures/NGS Images; 22, © Dan Burton/Alamy; 23, © Dave Houser/Photolibrary; 24, Courtesy Leanne Allison and Karsten Heuer/necessaryjourneys.ca; 25, © Patrick J. Endres/AlaskaPhotoGraphics.com; 26, © © John E. Marriott,wildernessprints.com; 27, © Stefan Meyers/Animals Animals Enterprises; 28, © Science Faction/SuperStock; 29T, © John E. Marriott,wildernessprints.com; 29B, © Konrad Wothe/Minden Pictures/NGS Images; 31, © Bryan Eastham/Shutterstock.

Publisher: Kenn Goin
Senior Editor: Lisa Wiseman
Creative Director: Spencer Brinker
Photo Researcher: Jennifer Bright

Library of Congress Cataloging-in-Publication Data

Markovics, Joyce L.
  Caribou: and reindeer, too / by Joyce Markovics.
     p. cm. — (Built for the cold — arctic animals)
  Includes bibliographical references and index.
  ISBN-13: 978-1-61772-130-4 (library binding)
  ISBN-10: 1-61772-130-1 (library binding)
  1. Caribou—Juvenile literature. 2. Reindeer—Juvenile literature. I. Title.
  QL737.U55M296 2011
  599.65'8—dc22
                              2010038854

For more information, write to Bearport Publishing Company, Inc., 101 Fifth Avenue, Suite 6R, New York, New York 10003. Printed in the United States of America in North Mankato, Minnesota.

122010
10810CGF

10 9 8 7 6 5 4 3 2 1

Contents

Caribou!

The fog was thick on the Firth River in northern Canada in June 2001. From the tiny window of a cabin, **biologist** Karsten Heuer watched the riverbank. Through a break in the fog, he saw a group of seven grizzly bears that had gathered near the river. What were they doing? he wondered.

A grizzly bear in northern Canada

A small group of caribou walking through fog

Using binoculars, Karsten peered at one of the bears in the distance. Then something on the slope behind the bear moved. Karsten struggled to make out what it was. Soon after, something much larger moved. "Suddenly the whole slope was alive," remembers Karsten. He finally realized what he was seeing. "Caribou!" he gasped.

The grizzly bears Karsten saw on the riverbank were waiting to attack and kill the caribou. In addition to bears, wolves and golden eagles hunt caribou.

Too Many to Count

At first, Karsten saw just a few hundred caribou. Then there were thousands winding through the valley. "Caribou dotted every hillside and the skyline," remembers Karsten. They raced across the dark, rocky slopes, their **hooves** pounding the ground. The noise from their running sounded like thunder.

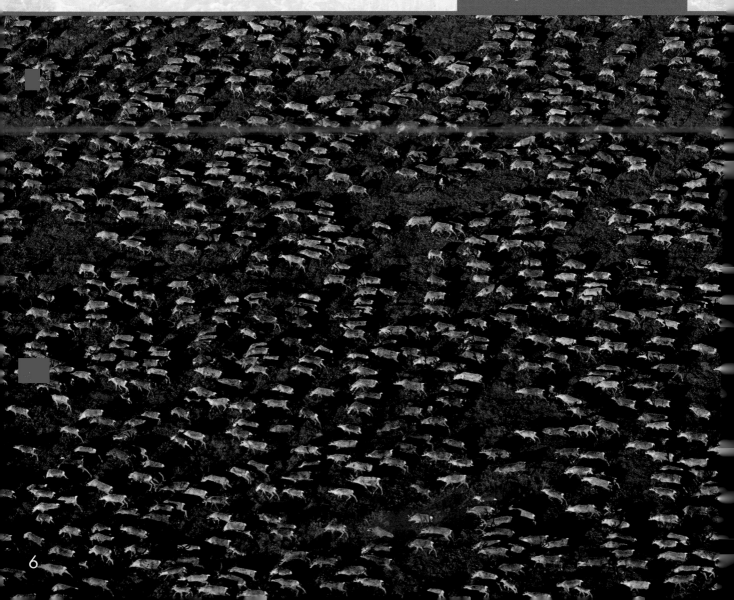

A group of caribou traveling through a valley

The next day Karsten wondered if he had imagined seeing the giant caribou **herd**. Had it all been a dream? Yet when he slipped his raft into the river, he saw the last few caribou moving out of the valley. Seeing the herd inspired Karsten to plan a trip to study them. He wanted to learn all about these animals and their struggle to survive in the **Arctic region**, one of the coldest places on Earth.

The caribou is a large **mammal** that stands four to five feet (1.2 to 1.5 m) tall at the shoulders. It's a member of the deer family.

An Incredible Mission

Caribou live throughout the freezing cold Arctic region, which includes northern areas of North America, Europe, and Asia. No one is exactly sure how many caribou there are, but scientists think there are between three and five million of the animals **roaming** these parts.

Caribou roaming Alaska

The caribou Karsten saw were part of the Porcupine caribou herd. Each spring, the thousands of caribou in the group **migrate** from their winter home near the Brooks Mountain Range in Alaska, traveling north more than 600 miles (966 km). Their long journey brings them back to a special area called the **calving grounds**, located on the plains and foothills of Alaska's Arctic National Wildlife Refuge and in parts of northern Canada. This is where the caribou give birth and begin to raise their young.

The Porcupine caribou herd is named after the Porcupine River, which runs through Alaska and Canada.

Where Caribou Live in the Wild

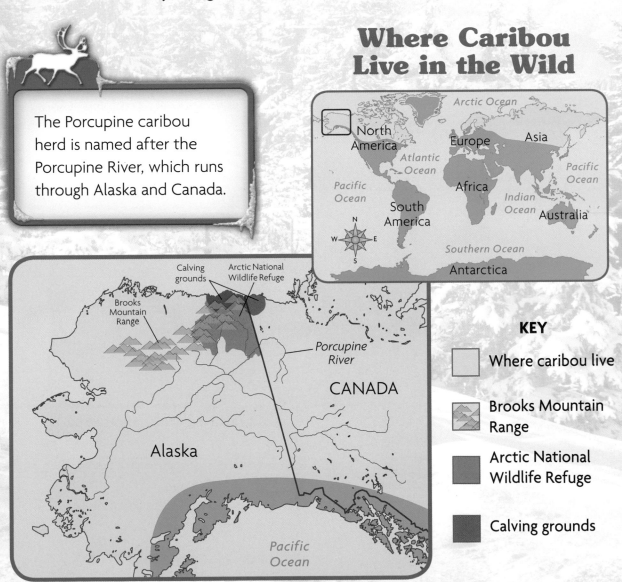

Arctic Ocean

North America

Europe

Asia

Atlantic Ocean

Pacific Ocean

Africa

Pacific Ocean

South America

Indian Ocean

Australia

N
W   E
S

Southern Ocean

Antarctica

Calving grounds

Arctic National Wildlife Refuge

Brooks Mountain Range

Porcupine River

CANADA

Alaska

Pacific Ocean

KEY

Where caribou live

Brooks Mountain Range

Arctic National Wildlife Refuge

Calving grounds

Obstacles Ahead

Beginning in April 2003, Karsten and his wife, Leanne Allison, a filmmaker, set off to follow the Porcupine herd on foot as the animals migrated. Their journey wouldn't be easy. To find the caribou herd, they would have to follow the animals' hoofprints. Then, once they located the caribou, they would have to move fast in order to keep up with the group. These animals travel fast. Adult caribou can **sprint** up to 30 miles per hour (48 kph). However, most of the time, they move by walking at a steady pace. Even so, they can still easily cover up to 20 miles (32 km) in one day!

Caribou use their long legs and strong muscles to cover a lot of ground quickly.

Each year, caribou travel about 3,000 miles (4,828 km)—about the distance from New York to California.

What's more, Karsten and Leanne would have to live in one of the most **treacherous** places on Earth—the Arctic **tundra**. This area is covered with frozen swamps, **mud bogs**, icy rivers, and steep, snow-covered mountains. Alongside the caribou, they would have to face snowstorms and bone-chilling cold. Even in spring, the temperature can drop below −35°F (−37°C).

The Arctic tundra is a mostly wide-open space that is home to wolves, bears, musk oxen, lemmings, arctic hares, and weasels, as well as caribou.

Leanne and Karsten, shown here, planned to carry all their supplies in huge backpacks that weighed from 60 to 80 pounds (27 to 36 kg).

Hooves and Hoofprints

In order to survive the freezing Arctic, Karsten and Leanne would have to bundle up in many layers of clothing, **Gore-Tex** jackets, and heavy boots. The caribou, however, needed no preparation for the Arctic temperatures. They are already **adapted** to life in the snow and bitter cold. For example, they have large, wide hooves that help them move without sinking into the snow too much. Also, the edges of their hooves are sharp, which helps them grip icy slopes.

The caribou's wide hooves are also great for paddling through icy water.

hollowed-out hoof

The word *caribou* comes from a Native American word that means "snow scraper." The animals were given this name because their hooves are hollowed out on the bottom like an ice cream scooper. They use their hollow hooves to dig into and scrape away the snow to find plants to eat.

Being **agile** helps caribou survive in the Arctic. They need to be able to zip through dense forests, along steep cliffs, and down icy slopes. Karsten and Leanne learned this firsthand as they ducked under tree branches and walked through deep snow while following a narrow trail of caribou hoofprints.

While Karsten and Leanne struggled to walk through deep snow, the caribou easily made their way through it.

Surviving the Cold

Caribou have adapted in other ways to life in the Arctic. Their bodies are covered with two layers of fur. In winter, the outer layer grows to be about three inches (8 cm) long. The hair is hollow, which allows it to trap warm air near the animal's body. The shorter layer of hair underneath also keeps the heat in. Even the caribou's lips and tail are covered with fur for warmth.

Caribou have furry coats to keep them warm.

The caribou's big, fuzzy nose plays a part in keeping the animal warm, too. Its **nostrils**, which are covered with fur, are able to heat up the cold air before it reaches the lungs. The caribou's nose is also useful in another way. The animal uses it to poke around in the snow to find food such as **lichens**, mosses, herbs, ferns, and grasses.

A caribou's nostrils are covered with soft fur.

A caribou sniffing for food under the snow

A caribou's sense of smell is so powerful that it can sniff out plants buried under five feet (1.5 m) of snow! Caribou also use their noses to sniff out enemies, such as wolves and bears.

Where Are the Caribou?

Several days into their **trek**, Karsten and Leanne had still seen only caribou hoofprints. Exhausted, they set up their tent for the night and fell asleep. Suddenly, they were woken up by a strange noise. Zipping open the tent, Karsten and Leanne were greeted by caribou—hundreds of them! Some even stopped to sniff around their tent.

Karsten and Leanne were following caribou hoofprints like these.

When a caribou walks, it makes a strange clicking noise. A **tendon** that slips over the caribou's foot bone causes this sound.

Karsten and Leanne were filled with excitement. They would now have a chance to travel along with the Porcupine herd. In all, there were more than 120,000 animals in the huge group. Caribou stick together for comfort and safety. However, there are usually a few at the front of a herd that lead the rest of the group.

Caribou are very social animals and like being around each other. Staying in large groups also helps keep them safe as they are less likely to be attacked by other animals.

Follow the Leaders

Most of the caribou passing by Karsten and Leanne's tent were females, called cows. Females and males, called bulls, look alike, but cows are about half the size of the largest bulls. Caribou are the only members of the deer family in which both the males and females have **antlers**. A bull's antlers are massive, growing up to five feet (1.5 m) long and weighing 33 pounds (15 kg). A cow's antlers are usually much smaller.

A male caribou

Males and females shed their antlers once a year. They grow new ones, which are bigger, a few months later.

A female caribou

During the spring and summer, a caribou's antlers, such as this one, are covered in a soft layer of skin called velvet. Each fall, after the antlers have grown, the velvet is shed.

During the migration, female and young caribou travel ahead of the males. The cows lead the group because they are in a hurry to reach the calving grounds to give birth to their young, called calves.

Two males fighting

Bulls use their large antlers to fight off other bulls. They also display them to the cows to show their strength.

The Calving Grounds

The cows usually reach the calving grounds at the end of May, after a month or two of travel. By this time of year, there's usually little snow on the ground and there are lots of plants for the caribou to eat. One adult caribou can eat about 12 pounds (5 kg) of food a day.

The calving grounds

The calving grounds are an ideal place for caribou families because there is plenty of food and there are few **predators**.

A female caribou delivers one calf each year. At birth, each calf weighs about 13 pounds (6 kg) and is a little larger than a football. Within minutes of being born, the long-legged calves are able to stand up on their own. By the next day, they're running around, trying to keep up with their mothers. Young caribou grow very fast, doubling their weight in just 10 to 15 days!

A mother caribou from the Porcupine herd tries to help her newborn calf stand.

A caribou calf from the Porcupine herd standing on its own

21

Caribou or Reindeer?

Unlike the wild animals that Karsten and Leanne were following, another type of caribou, known as reindeer, lives closely with people. Caribou and reindeer are the same **species**, but reindeer are **domesticated**. They are also often smaller and have shorter legs than caribou.

Reindeer and caribou look alike, except reindeer are smaller.

Experts believe that reindeer were first domesticated between 3,000 and 7,000 years ago.

Reindeer live in northern Russia and northern Europe. In northern Europe, some of the Sami people of **Lapland**, as well as some people in Russia, follow their herds as the animals move between summer and winter feeding areas. When the reindeer are not feeding, people use them to pull sleds. The Sami also rely on reindeer meat for food and use their skins for clothing.

Some Sami people use reindeer to help them pull sleds.

A Place to Call Home

After a jouney of about 1,000 miles (1,609 km) with the Porcupine caribou herd to the calving grounds and back, Karsten and Leanne had learned a lot. Apart from gaining a deep appreciation of what it takes to survive in the Arctic, they realized how important it is to protect the places where caribou live and raise their young.

Leanne, shown here, and Karsten spent five months in the Arctic wilderness following the Porcupine herd.

Some caribou **habitats** are under serious threat. For example, the Porcupine herd's calving grounds are located in an area of the Arctic National Wildlife Refuge that contains **oil**, which some companies want to **extract**. To allow oil drilling there could force the caribou to find a new calving area. Karsten thinks that could mean "a decline in the herd, perhaps even forcing them into extinction."

Oil and gas pipelines may block or disrupt the caribou's migration routes.

Male caribou can live to be 10 years or older in the wild. Female caribou often live a few years longer.

Keeping Caribou Wild

Humans are harming the caribou's habitat in other ways, too. They are cutting down forests and building roads where caribou live and roam. To survive, these animals need huge areas in which they can move freely. Without enough land, caribou might not be able to escape from predators, find the food they need to survive, and migrate to and from their feeding and calving grounds.

In some areas of Canada and the United States, caribou are considered **threatened** or **endangered**.

Sometimes caribou are hit by cars as they cross roads built in areas where they live.

Even though Karsten and Leanne are no longer following the caribou, they have not forgotten their hoofed friends. After their trip, they traveled to Washington, D.C., to meet with members of Congress to raise awareness about caribou and their future. Their hope is that by letting people know about these amazing Arctic animals, the caribou will continue forever, as Karsten says, "in ways that are wild and free."

Leanne made a film, called *Being Caribou* (2005), about her and Karsten's amazing adventure with the animals.

Caribou Facts

Caribou are perfectly suited to life in freezing temperatures. Their bodies are covered with two layers of fur to keep them warm. Caribou also have large, wide hooves, which help them walk and dig in snow and paddle through icy water. Here are some other facts about these amazing animals.

Weight:	males weigh 220 to 700 pounds (100 to 318 kg); females weigh 130 to 370 pounds (59 to 168 kg)
Height:	four to five feet (1.2 to 1.5 m) tall at the shoulders
Food:	grasses, lichens, mosses, and herbs
Life Span:	10 years or more in the wild for males; a few years longer for females
Habitat:	Arctic region
Population:	Scientists don't have an exact number, but they think there are between three and five million caribou in the wild.

More Arctic Animals

The caribou is only one kind of animal that lives in the Arctic. There are many other animals living there that have also adapted in order to survive the extreme cold. Here are two of them.

Grizzly Bear

- Grizzly bears are huge—weighing up to 551 pounds (250 kg)! In spite of this, they're fast and can run up to 30 miles per hour (48 kph).
- With an appetite to match their size, grizzly bears will eat everything from berries and nuts to other animals, including fish, rodents, caribou, and moose.

- Grizzly bears are relatives of black bears, which live in North America.

Golden Eagle

- The golden eagle is the largest **bird of prey** in North America, with a six-to-seven-foot (1.8-to-2.1-m) wingspan.

- Golden eagles use their sharp **talons** to hunt marmots, ground squirrels, and caribou calves. They can dive at more than 150 miles per hour (241 kph) to catch their prey.
- They're called golden eagles because they have gold feathers on their heads and necks. The rest of their body is brown.

29

Glossary

adapted (uh-DAPT-tid) changed over time to survive in an environment

agile (AJ-il) able to move around fast and easily

antlers (ANT-lurz) large bony, branching structures that grow out of some animals' heads, such as caribou and deer

Arctic region (ARK-tic REE-juhn) the northernmost area on Earth; it includes the Arctic Ocean, the North Pole, and northern parts of Europe, Asia, and North America; one of the coldest areas in the world

biologist (bye-OL-uh-jist) a scientist who studies plants or animals

bird of prey (BIRD UHV PRAY) a bird that hunts other animals for food

calving grounds (KAV-ing groundz) an area of land where caribou give birth

domesticated (duh-MESS-tuh-*kate*-id) animals that have been tamed so that they can live with people

endangered (en-DAYN-jurd) being in danger of dying out

extract (ek-STRAKT) to remove something

Gore-Tex (GOR-teks) a waterproof material used in outdoor clothing

habitats (HAB-uh-*tats*) places in nature where plants or animals normally live

herd (HURD) a large group of animals

hooves (HOOVZ) hard coverings over the feet of some animals such as caribou and horses

Lapland (LAP-land) a cold area in northern Europe

lichens (LYE-kuhnz) flat moss-like growths on rocks and trees

mammal (MAM-uhl) a warm-blooded animal that has a backbone, has hair or fur on its skin, and drinks its mother's milk as a baby

migrate (MYE-grate) to move from one place to another at a certain time of the year

mud bogs (MUHD BOGZ) areas of soft, wet land

nostrils (NOSS-truhlz) two openings in the nose that are used for breathing and smelling

oil (OIL) a thick liquid that is used to heat homes and make gas for cars

predators (PRED-uh-turz) animals that hunt other animals for food

roaming (ROHM-ing) wandering around

species (SPEE-sheez) groups that animals are divided into according to similar characteristics; members of the same species can have offspring together

sprint (SPRINT) to run fast for a short distance

talons (TAL-uhnz) the sharp claws of a bird

tendon (TEN-duhn) a strong, thick cord that joins muscle to bone

threatened (THRET-uhnd) having an uncertain chance of surviving

treacherous (TRECH-ur-uhss) very dangerous or hazardous

trek (TREK) a slow, difficult journey

tundra (TUHN-druh) cold, treeless land where the ground is always frozen just below the surface

Bibliography

Heuer, Karsten. *Being Caribou: Five Months on Foot with an Arctic Herd.* Minneapolis, MN: Milkweed Editions (2005).

Alaska Department of Fish & Game
(www.adfg.state.ak.us/pubs/notebook/biggame/caribou.php)

U.S. Fish & Wildlife Service, Arctic National Wildlife Refuge
(arctic.fws.gov/carcon.htm)

Wildlife Conservation Society
(www.wcs.org/saving-wildlife/hoofed-mammals/caribou.aspx)

Read More

Miller, Debbie S. *A Caribou Journey.* Fairbanks, AK: University of Alaska Press (2010).

Somervill, Barbara A. *Animal Survivors of the Arctic.* New York: Scholastic Library (2004).

Vogel, Julia. *Caribou (Our Wild World).* Chanhassan, MN: NorthWord Books for Young Readers (2002).

Learn More Online

To learn more about caribou, visit
www.bearportpublishing.com/BuiltforCold

Index

About the Author

Joyce Markovics is an editor, writer, and orchid collector. She lives with her husband, Adam, in New York City, far from the incredible roaming caribou of the frozen Arctic.